I KNOW AMERICA

Our National Holidays

Karen Spies

THE MILLBROOK PRESS
Brookfield, Connecticut

Published by The Millbrook Press
2 Old New Milford Road
Brookfield, CT 06804
© 1992 Blackbirch Graphics, Inc.
First Edition

Created and produced in association with Blackbirch Graphics.
Series Editor: Bruce S. Glassman

pbk: 10 9 8 7 6 5 4
lib: 10 9 8 7 6 5 4 3 2

Library of Congress Cataloging-in-Publication Data

Spies, Karen Bornemann
    Our national holidays / Karen Spies.
    Includes bibliographical references and index.
    Summary: Examines the history and significance of patriotic holidays,
holidays that honor famous people, and special American holidays such as
Thanksgiving.
    ISBN 1-878841-88-2 (pbk.)
    1. Holidays—United States—Juvenile literature. [1. Holidays.] I. Title.
II. Series.
GT2703.S66   1992
394.2'6'0973—dc20   91-38894
                                                                       CIP
                                                                        AC

Acknowledgments and Photo Credits

Cover: ©Stacy Pick/Stock, Boston, Inc.; Back cover courtesy of the U.S.
Naval Academy, Annapolis, Maryland; p. 4: ©Frank Siteman/Stock, Boston,
Inc.; p. 7: ©Owen Franken/Stock, Boston, Inc.; pp. 8, 9, 20, 23, 35, 43:
Library of Congress Collection; pp. 11, 40: ©Bob Daemmrich/The Image
Works; p. 12: ©William Clark/Courtesy Department of the Interior; p. 14:
private collection; p. 16: Wide World Photos, Inc.; p. 19: UPI/Bettmann
Newsphotos; pp. 21, 32: Bettmann; p. 24: North Wind Picture Archives;
p. 26: ©Ron Edmonds/Wide World photos; p. 28: ©Richard Vogel/Gamma-
Liaison; p. 29: ©Scott Robinson/Stock South; p. 31: ©Rick Bowmer/Wide
World Photos; p. 38: Denver Partnership; p. 39: ©Andrea Wade; p. 44:
©Chiasson/Gamma-Liaison.

Photo Research by **Inge King.**

23456789

CONTENTS

CHAPTER 1 **What Is a National Holiday?**   **5**

CHAPTER 2 **Celebrating Our Nation's Roots**   **9**

Independence Day   9
Flag Day   11
Labor Day   13
Citizenship Day   14

CHAPTER 3 **Honoring Famous People**   **17**

Martin Luther King, Jr., Day   17
Washington's Birthday   20
Lincoln's Birthday   20
Columbus Day   22

CHAPTER 4 **Honoring Our Armed Forces**   **27**

Memorial Day   27
Veterans Day   30

CHAPTER 5 **Celebrating Our Heritage**   **33**

Thanksgiving Day   33
Chinese New Year   36
Cinco de Mayo   38
Kwanzaa   38
Native American Day   39

CHAPTER 6 **Celebrating Our Earth**   **41**

Arbor Day   41
Bird Day   42
Earth Day   44

Chronology   **46**
For Further Reading   **46**
Index   **47**

WHAT IS A NATIONAL HOLIDAY?

When you hear the word *holiday,* what comes to mind? Time off from school? Fireworks? Parades? Picnics? Just what is a holiday, anyway? And what do we mean when we use the term *national holiday?*

The word *holiday* comes from the Old English words *halig daeg,* meaning "holy day." Today, a holiday takes place when we set aside a special time to honor an important person or event. It might be a religious holiday, such as Easter. Or a patriotic holiday, such as Independence Day (July Fourth). But how does a holiday become a *national* holiday?

A national holiday is set aside by law and celebrated nationwide. In the United States of

Opposite:
A young girl lights sparklers in Massachusetts to help celebrate Independence Day.

America, there are no true national holidays. That is because the governor of each state has the power to set aside the holidays for that state. But we think of holidays like July Fourth and Memorial Day as national holidays. That is because every state in the country always celebrates them.

In this book, you will read about the history and observance of many different holidays. These holidays may honor:

- an important event in our nation's history
- a famous person from America's past
- our armed forces
- our diverse ethnic heritage
- the natural world around us

Each of these holidays is different from the others. Some, such as Memorial Day and Fourth of July, are legal, or public, holidays. Banks, schools, and some businesses close on legal holidays. Except for the Fourth of July, these holidays are usually observed on specific days of the week, most often on Mondays.

Other holidays, such as Flag Day, are set aside by presidential proclamation (order). You may not get to stay home from school on these holidays, but they are still important times to honor traditions from our country's past.

Each national holiday has something that is very important in common with the others: They all have to do with our country and its traditions. Each holiday celebrates America's past, present, and future. That is why we think of them as our national holidays.

Children march in a patriotic Flag Day parade through the streets of Boston, Massachusetts.

CHAPTER 2

CELEBRATING OUR NATION'S ROOTS

A flag waves gently in the breeze. Fireworks explode on the Fourth of July. Crowds sing "The Star-Spangled Banner" at a big sports event. All these things are symbols of our nation. They are part of the ways in which we honor our country. In this chapter, we will talk about holidays that honor important events in American history.

Independence Day: July Fourth

Independence Day honors the day that the American colonies adopted the Declaration of Independence: July 4, 1776. The colonies declared themselves independent from England and its king, George III.

Opposite:
The adoption of the Declaration of Independence, July 4, 1776.

Since 1775, the colonists had been at war with England. The two sides were fighting because the British government had forced the colonists to sell their tobacco, wood, and furs only to Britain. And the colonists had to get many goods from Britain and other countries. Britain was nearly 3,500 miles away. It took a long time for goods to reach the colonies. To make matters worse, Britain's Parliament taxed the colonists without giving them a say in how they were taxed.

In America, the Continental Congress met and appointed a committee to write a Declaration of Independence. This would say that America was no longer under British control. The committee included John Adams, Benjamin Franklin, and Thomas Jefferson. Jefferson wrote the first draft of the Declaration in two and one-half weeks.

The founders of the new country knew that the July Fourth signing day would be a great day of rejoicing for years to come. John Adams wrote that he expected the day to be marked by parades, games, sports, balls, and bonfires, from one end of the continent to the other.

Independence Day was first celebrated on July 4, 1777, in Philadelphia, which was the capital at the time. In honor of the celebration, warships along the docks fired their cannons. Bells were rung and bands played. At night, bonfires and fireworks lit up the skies. Since that day, the Fourth of July has been celebrated each year throughout the country.

Thomas Jefferson wrote the first draft of the Declaration of Independence in two and one-half weeks.

Many important events in our country's history have taken place on the Fourth. The United States Military Academy at West Point was opened on July 4, 1802. In 1850, the cornerstone of the Washington Monument in Washington, D.C., was laid down on the Fourth of July. The Phillipine Islands, which had been a United States territory, got their first American governor on July 4, 1903.

A young boy celebrates July Fourth in a special way.

Flag Day: June 14

Our flag was born on June 14, 1777. That is when the Continental Congress said that the flag of the thirteen United States should be thirteen red and white stripes, with thirteen white stars in a blue field. As the nation grew, a star and a stripe were added for each new state. Soon the flag was in danger of becoming too large. In 1818, Congress decided that the flag would return to its original thirteen stripes, but that a star would be added for each new state. Today the flag has fifty white stars.

The flag was one hundred years old before a special celebration was established in its honor. In 1877, Congress declared that the flag should be flown over public buildings on June 14. In 1889, New York City schools celebrated a day in honor of the flag. Gradually the idea spread. In 1914, President Woodrow Wilson asked that Flag Day be observed throughout the nation. In 1949, Congress officially named June 14 as Flag Day.

GETTING A BANG OUT OF FIREWORKS

Fireworks displays use explosive shells. The shells range in size from two inches to three feet in diameter. They can weigh up to seven hundred pounds. The shells are usually fired from big steels tubes called mortars. If you think of fireworks being shot like a gun, the mortar acts as the gun barrel and the shells are the bullets.

A fireworks shell is a brown paper tube filled with special chemicals. Six or seven layers of paper are glued together to form a tube. A layer of gunpowder is placed at the bottom and the top of each tube, with chunks and lumps of chemicals in between. These special chemicals give fireworks their bright colors and sparks.

A fuse of woven threads extends from the top of the tube. The fuse must be cut to exactly the right length so that the firework will explode in the air, not on the ground. When the fuse is lit, the gunpowder catches fire. Escaping gases propel the shell into the air.

A large shell can be designed to explode in several stages, or "breaks." Each break can be a different color and can explode with a loud noise. Different chemicals packed inside the shell create different colors and effects. The following is a list of colors and the chemicals that produce them when they explode:

Red: strontium or lithium
Blue: copper
Yellow: sodium
Orange: charcoal or iron
Green: barium
White: aluminum powder or
    magnesium
Sulfur is added to black powder to make the loud boom and bright flash that are the finale of many fireworks displays.

Today, Flag Day is celebrated in many schools. The celebrations usually include speeches, singing of patriotic songs, and pledging allegiance to the flag. The author of the pledge is generally thought to be Francis Bellamy. The pledge was first published in the *Youth's Companion* magazine in 1892. We pledge allegiance to the flag because it stands for America.

Labor Day: First Monday in September

The first Labor Day celebration was held in New York City on September 5, 1882. It was suggested by Peter J. McGuire, founder of the United Brotherhood of Carpenters.

In the 1880s and 1890s, relations between workers and managers were often bitter. Workers toiled twelve to fourteen hours a day, seven days a week, in dirty, unsafe buildings. Many children had to go to work at age eleven or twelve. McGuire's Brotherhood was one of many labor unions, or workers' organizations, created to help workers gain fair pay and safer working conditions.

McGuire wanted factory workers to feel pride in their jobs. And he wanted them to be honored for their hard work. A parade and picnic were planned. More than ten thousand workers participated in the first Labor Day parade. After the parade, 50,000 people filled a nearby park. They heard speeches about how to form unions and end child labor. They enjoyed playing games, and eating a picnic together. They made the first Labor Day a huge success.

Peter McGuire was the first to suggest the idea of Labor Day, around 1882.

Soon other states declared their own holidays in honor of workers. Today, all fifty states observe Labor Day.

The holiday has taken on different meanings since McGuire's time. Because Labor Day is always a Monday, many people enjoy a three-day weekend on this holiday. For most people this weekend signals the end of summer.

Most American workers today earn fairer wages than did workers in McGuire's day. Working conditions are now cleaner and safer. But the idea of honoring workers and the jobs they do still continues.

Citizenship Day: September 17

This holiday combines two holidays that no longer exist: I Am an American Day and Constitution Day. I Am an American Day was suggested by members of the American Legion at their 1940 convention in Boston. They wanted to honor foreigners who had just become new citizens.

Constitution Day was formally celebrated on September 17, the anniversary of the signing of the Constitution in 1787. America had won its freedom from Great Britain. The new country needed a constitution—a set of basic laws around which to organize the government. It took the writers of the Constitution four months to agree on a final draft. It was approved by a majority of the states and came into effect as the law of the land on March 4, 1789.

Since its signing, the Constitution has been changed very little. Only twenty-six amendments, or changes, have been added in the more than two hundred years since the Constitution was signed.

The Constitution protects the rights of all our citizens, including the very newest ones. It made sense to combine a holiday honoring the Constitution with a holiday honoring new citizens. In 1952, Constitution Day and I Am an American Day were joined into one holiday: Citizenship Day. It is observed on September 17, the anniversary of the signing of the Constitution. The week beginning September 17 and ending September 23 is known as Constitution Week.

Patriotic celebrations mark both Citizenship Day and Constitution Week. Schools study the importance of citizenship and its role in our government under the Constitution. Programs usually include speeches, the singing of patriotic songs, and the reciting of the Pledge of Allegiance. Days are set aside during the week for new citizens to take the oath of allegiance to their new country, the United States.

Special ceremonies took place in 1987, on the two hundredth anniversary of the signing of the Consititution. On September 17, at 4:00 P.M., the time of the signing of the Constitution, a model of the Liberty Bell was rung in Philadelphia. At the same time, people throughout the United States joined in ringing bells and chimes. This Bells Across America ceremony has since become a tradition in many American communities.

HONORING
FAMOUS PEOPLE

America observes holidays that honor four people who have played an important part in our country's history: Martin Luther King, Jr., George Washington, Abraham Lincoln, and Christopher Columbus.

Martin Luther King, Jr., Day:
Third Monday in January

Martin Luther King, Jr., had a dream: He wanted the laws of our land applied in the same way to all people. Our newest legal holiday honors this famous civil rights leader, who was born on January 15, 1929, in Atlanta, Georgia.

Opposite:
Martin Luther King, Jr., led the fight for civil rights in America during the 1960s.

When Martin Luther King, Jr., was growing up, blacks in the south were victims of segregation (keeping blacks separate from whites). Blacks had to give their bus seats to whites. Blacks could not use the whites' public rest rooms, drink out of the same drinking fountains, or stay in the same hotels. The schools for black children were in poor condition and had fewer books and materials than schools for white children. Blacks could not buy houses in white areas. Often, good jobs were not open to them. Whites also made it hard for blacks to vote.

Martin Luther King, Jr., believed in using only nonviolent ways to end segregation. In 1955, he led a bus boycott in Montgomery, Alabama. Rosa Parks, a black woman, had recently been arrested for refusing to give up her bus seat to a white person. For a year, boycotters refused to ride city buses until the unfair law was changed.

In 1957, King founded the Southern Christian Leadership Conference (SCLC), which helped many blacks register to vote. He also united blacks and whites in many nonviolent protests and marches, such as the famous March on Washington. It took place August 28, 1963. At the march, King gave his historic speech entitled "I Have a Dream."

Because King worked to change laws through nonviolent means, he won the Nobel Peace Prize in 1963. Partly through King's efforts, the Voting Rights Act was passed in 1965. It made illegal some of the practices that had prevented blacks from voting.

Unfortunately, feelings about segregation were still strong. Sometimes fighting took place between police and civil rights protestors. Violence kept Martin Luther King, Jr., from fulfilling his dream of equal rights. He was shot and killed on April 4, 1968, outside his hotel room in Memphis, Tennessee.

Fifteen years after his death, King's birthday became a legal holiday. It is celebrated on the third Monday of January. On this day, Americans have an opportunity to remember his efforts and honor the goal of equal rights for all our citizens.

Rosa Parks sparked the early fight for civil rights when she refused to give up her seat on a bus to a white person.

George Washington led American troops to victory in the Revolutionary War against the British.

Washington's Birthday: Third Monday in February

George Washington was commander in chief of the army during the Revolutionary War against the British. As our first president, he served two terms, from 1789 to 1796. Because of his leadership role in America's history, he is known as "the father of our country."

After the Revolution, Washington's birthday, February 22, became an important holiday. During colonial times, Americans had observed the birthday of the king of England. Now the new nation wanted to honor its own hero. Balls and parades marked the first celebration, held in Richmond, Virginia. It was not until 1800, the year after his death, that Washington's birthday was observed nationally.

Today, schools, banks, and government offices are closed on Washington's Birthday. A wreath is laid on Washington's tomb at Mount Vernon, his Virginia plantation. In Valley Forge, Pennsylvania, there is a re-enactment of Washington's army encampment during the winter of 1778.

All over the United States, we have honored George Washington in many ways. Our nation's capital, a state, and many cities are named after him. The Washington Monument in our nation's capital is a tribute to the memory of this great leader.

Lincoln's Birthday: Third Monday in February

Only nine years after Washington's death, another famous American was born. He worked to save the nation that George Washington had helped to found. This man, Abraham Lincoln, served as our sixteenth president, from 1861 through 1865.

Abe Lincoln was born in a small log cabin near Hodgenville, Kentucky, on February 12, 1809. He went to school for just one year. But because he loved to read, Lincoln became well educated.

In the 1850s, the practice of slavery divided America between North and South. Most people in the Northern States were in favor of stopping (abolishing) slavery. Southerners depended on slaves to work the plantations and cotton fields. They did not want slavery abolished. This conflict led to the Civil War, in which the North was pitted against the South. Lincoln was president during the Civil War. Like many Northerners, he was against owning and selling slaves. Most Southerners wanted to continue slavery. Slaves provided cheap labor for the cotton industry.

The many deaths caused by the Civil War saddened President Lincoln. But he was determined to keep the country whole. In 1863, Lincoln issued the famous Emancipation Proclamation, which freed the slaves. Two years later, the Thirteenth Amendment to the Constitution made slavery illegal. On November 19, 1863, he gave his famous Gettysburg Address. In that speech Lincoln expressed his faith that all Americans would be free.

On April 9, 1865, the South surrendered. Lincoln wanted to heal the differences between the North and South. But his dream was not to be. Five

Abraham Lincoln delivered his Gettysburg Address on November 19, 1863, during the Civil War.

days after the war's end, John Wilkes Booth shot the president in Ford's Theatre in Washington, D.C.

Beginning with the first year after Lincoln's death, his birthday was observed at a special combined meeting of the House and Senate. In 1892, the state of Illinois, where Lincoln had lived for many years, made February 12 a state holiday. Soon other states followed the example of Illinois. Today, Lincoln's birthday is usually celebrated with Washington's birthday on the third Monday in February. This holiday is now commonly called Presidents' Day.

Columbus Day: Second Monday in October

Columbus Day is important not only to people in the United States, but also to residents of Canada and Central and South America. It is a day to honor the brave Italian explorer who sailed across the Atlantic Ocean to North and South America.

At the time Columbus lived, most educated people knew that the world was round. But they still thought it was much smaller than it is. Columbus wanted to prove that one could sail a different route to the East Indies. He hoped to find a shorter route to the East Indies, where traders went for spices and silks. He soon convinced Queen Isabella and King Ferdinand of Spain to give him three ships: The *Niña*, the *Pinta*, and the *Santa María*.

By October 10, 1492, the ships had been sailing for about five weeks without any sight of land.

Everyone agreed to sail for three more days and then turn back if land was not sighted. At two in the morning on October 12, a lookout spotted land. At daybreak, Columbus landed on an island, one of the islands that are now known as the Bahamas. His success in reaching the "New World" would later encourage other explorers. And it proved to even simple people that the world was not flat.

Christopher Columbus was a brave explorer whose journeys opened the way for other navigators and explorers.

Before Columbus arrived, Native Americans had lived in North America for hundreds of years. Most Indians lived in highly organized villages.

In America, Columbus Day was first celebrated as a holiday in 1792 in New York City. This was the three hundredth anniversary of his landing. In 1934, President Franklin D. Roosevelt made October 12 a legal holiday.

Today, Columbus Day is usually celebrated on the second Monday in October. It is observed in most states and in Puerto Rico. Likewise, Canada, countries in Central and South America, Italy, and Spain all honor the skilled navigator and explorer whose courage and determination helped to make his dream come true.

DID COLUMBUS DISCOVER A *NEW* WORLD?

Christopher Columbus is given credit for the discovery of a "New World." But for the many people who were living there before Columbus's arrival, North America was not "new" at all. In fact, Native Americans had already been living on the North and South American continents for centuries.

Other Europeans had even explored North America before Columbus. Some people think that in the eighth century, Irish monks sailed skin-covered boats across the ocean to Iceland. In the following century, Norwegian Vikings settled Iceland and discovered the vast area of Greenland.

In 985, Erik the Red established the first colony in Greenland. His son, Leif Eriksson, became the first to explore more of North America. Around the year 1000, Leif Eriksson first sighted what is believed to be present-day Newfoundland. He sailed along the coast as far south as Cape Cod, in present-day Massachusetts. He named the area Vinland because of the grapes he found growing there.

Why don't the Vikings and Leif Eriksson get the credit for "discovering" North America? That is because, even though the Vikings made maps of the area, they never made permanent settlements there. And they did not tell other nations about their discoveries. Christopher Columbus, when he landed in the "New World" almost five hundred years later, had never heard of Leif Eriksson or the Viking journeys.

CHAPTER 4

HONORING
OUR ARMED FORCES

Americans observe two important military holidays each year: Memorial Day and Veterans Day. Many people also observe Armed Forces Day on the third Saturday in May. On Armed Forces Day, members of the military put on special programs for citizens.

Memorial Day: Last Monday in May or May 30

It was April 26, 1866. The Civil War had ended the year before, but memories of the bitter battles lived on in the South. The women of Columbus, Mississippi, marched to the town cemetery. They decorated the graves of both Confederate and Union soldiers who had died in the war. They felt the men of both sides

Opposite:
A soldier places several flags of remembrance on the graves at Arlington National Cemetery.

had died for causes they believed to be right. A story about their surprising act was published in the *New York Herald Tribune*, where it attracted national interest. Today many people think that the Columbus women began the holiday we now celebrate as Memorial Day.

Other people believe Memorial Day began in Boalsburg, Pennsylvania. There, in 1864, Emma Hunter put flowers on her father's tomb. He had been a colonel in the Union Army. At the cemetery, she met another woman, whose son had died in the war. The two agreed to meet at the cemetery the following year to decorate the graves of their loved ones.

Still other people say the first Memorial Day was held in Waterloo, New York, on May 5, 1866. On that day, the entire village held a special Memorial Day celebration. Later, Waterloo was officially designated by Congress as the "birthplace" of Memorial Day.

The Grand Army of the Republic (GAR) was the first group to suggest that May 30 be set aside as a day to decorate the graves of Union soldiers. (The GAR was the Union veterans' association.) In 1868, the GAR organized a special ceremony at the National Cemetery in Arlington, Virginia, and called the observance Decoration Day. Several other nearby communities soon took up the idea. Eventually, the observance became known as Memorial Day.

Memorial Day has become a special time to remember American soldiers who have died in war. It is a legal holiday in Washington, D.C., Puerto Rico,

A large wreath of remembrance sits in front of the Vietnam War Memorial in Washington, D.C.

A member of the
Jewish War
Veterans salutes the
flag at a ceremony
in Atlanta, Georgia.

and most states. It is celebrated on either May 30 or
the last Monday in May. In the South, many states also
celebrate Confederate Memorial Day, honoring the
soldiers who fought for the Confederacy.

Today, parades of bands and soldiers mark most
Memorial Day observances. Services are held on ships
for those who died fighting at sea.

Veterans Day: November 11

World War I started in 1914. It pitted the Allies (France, Great Britain, Russia, Italy, and the United States) against Germany and its supporters. The Allies fought the war to stop Germany from taking over many other countries in Europe.

It was on November 11, 1918, that World War I finally ended. Germany and the Allies signed an agreement to stop fighting. An Australian journalist, George Honey, called for the world to keep silence for two minutes as the agreement was signed. Even radio broadcasts stopped (there was no television then). This tradition became known as the Great Silence. It is an important part of what has become our Veterans Day celebration.

At first, the holiday was known as Armistice Day. (An armistice is a cease-fire before the signing of a peace treaty; that is what the agreement signed on November 11, 1919, was.) In 1954, the observance was renamed Veterans Day.

On Veterans Day, many homes display blue and gold stars in their windows. These stars represent soldiers from that family who fought in a war. A blue star stands for a soldier who is living. A gold star means that the soldier died.

Many cities observe Veterans Day with parades of veterans from all American wars. Veterans also sell small red poppies, which represent the wild flowers that grew in the European battlefields in World War I.

REMEMBERING THOSE WHO ARE UNKNOWN

A solemn ceremony takes place on Veterans Day at National Cemetery in Arlington, Virginia. The president and other leaders lay a wreath on the Tomb of the Unknowns. This tomb was established in 1921. Written on it are the words:

HERE RESTS IN HONORED GLORY
AN AMERICAN SOLDIER
KNOWN BUT TO GOD

An unidentified soldier was selected to represent all those who had died in World War I. On November 11, 1921, at 11:00 A.M., the body was lowered into the tomb. Today the tomb also includes unknown soldiers from World War II, the Korean War, and the Vietnam War. Thousands of people from all over the world visit this memorial each year.

A special guard marches up the steps to the Tomb of the Unknowns.

CELEBRATING OUR HERITAGE

As this land's first residents, Native Americans celebrate a rich heritage of culture, including dance, folklore, and arts and crafts. The United States also has many citizens who have moved here from a variety of different countries. They brought with them their own customs, many of which they celebrate here. This chapter describes several of the holidays that honor our varied American heritage.

Thanksgiving: Fourth Thursday in November

A turkey stands with its feathers fanned out. A spicy pumpkin pie sits cooling on a windowsill. Pilgrims

Opposite:
Pilgrims and Indians feasted together at the very first Thanksgiving in the Plymouth Colony, 1621.

and Native Americans feast together at a giant table. All these are symbols of Thanksgiving Day.

Thanksgiving is a legal holiday, observed on the fourth Thursday of November. It is also a uniquely American holiday, closely tied to the history of our nation. Other countries honor national heroes and historical days. Many observe Christmas and New Year's Day. But only a few have a national day of thanksgiving.

The idea of giving thanks is not new, nor is it especially American. The Hebrews, Greeks, and Romans celebrated harvest festivals. In the Middle Ages and later, English Christians had them too. In the 1620s, the Pilgrims created a harvest festival to give thanks to God for a bounty of food.

The first Thanksgiving was observed in 1621. Governor Bradford of the Plymouth Colony set aside three days for feasting and giving thanks for the Pilgrims' successful harvest.

The tradition of Thanksgiving Day spread from Plymouth to other New England colonies. During the Revolutionary War, eight special days of thanksgiving were observed. Then President George Washington proclaimed November 26, 1789, as a national day to give thanks.

For a time, Thanksgiving was not celebrated yearly. Then, in 1846, Sarah Josepha Hale, editor of *Godey's Lady's Book*, began to promote the idea of a national day of thanks. She wrote about her idea in her magazine and sent many letters to the president. Finally, in 1863, President Abraham Lincoln proclaimed that the last Thursday of November should be set aside as a day for giving thanks.

Thanksgiving was celebrated in a way similar to the Pilgrims' feast. Pumpkins and cranberries (both distinctly American foods) became the symbols of a plentiful harvest. Americans joined with family and friends to feast on turkey and other native treats.

The day after Thanksgiving soon became known as the beginning of the Christmas shopping season. From 1939 through 1941, President Franklin Roosevelt proclaimed that Thanksgiving be celebrated on the *third* Thursday of November. That was because the last Thursday came very late in the month in those years. Moving Thanksgiving back gave merchants more time to sell Christmas merchandise.

Sara Josepha Hale led the fight to make Thanksgiving a national holiday.

Unfortunately, this change became a political issue. President Roosevelt was a Democrat. Republicans accused him of trying to change tradition. After two years, a compromise was reached: Thanksgiving was to be kept on the fourth Thursday in November.

Today, many cities have big Thanksgiving Day parades. The most famous is the traditional Macy's parade in New York City. During this long, elaborate procession, costumed characters from movies, books, and television stroll down the streets. They are often accompanied by colorful marching bands and decorated floats.

Chinese New Year: Various Days

The Chinese New Year is known as *Yuan Tan.* It is celebrated by Chinese people throughout the world, including Chinese Americans. While it is not always on the same date, Chinese New Year always falls somewhere between January 21 and February 19. The festivities last for fifteen days.

Before New Year's Day, children help their families clean the house and put up decorations. Red is considered a lucky color, so many red flowers are used to decorate the rooms. Red scrolls wish everyone prosperity and happiness in the year to come.

On New Year's Day, Chinese shops and businesses close. Families gather to celebrate. A special New Year meal usually includes dumplings with nuts and sugar. Parents give their children presents such as small red envelopes of "lucky money," which they use to buy holiday treats.

Fireworks are a big part of the celebration. The Chinese have long believed that evil spirits are around at the New Year. Firecrackers are supposed to scare the evil spirits away.

Traditionally, in China, the celebration ends with the Lantern Festival. Children and their families carry lighted paper lanterns through the streets. Clowns, musicians, and dancers also join the parade. There is always a Chinese dragon, the symbol of strength and good luck. It is made from lengths of bamboo covered with colored cloth or paper. Some dragons are more than a hundred feet long.

A CALENDAR OF ANIMALS

The date for the Chinese New Year is determined by the Chinese lunar calendar. The Chinese calendar is different from the American calendar. The Chinese calendar has been around since at least 1500 B.C. In this calendar, months are marked by the moon, but the year as a whole is measured by the sun. A new moon marks the beginning of each month. A full moon marks the middle of the month. The Chinese New Year is the first day of the first month of the lunar calendar. It falls sometime between January 21 and February 19.

The Chinese name each year after one of twelve animals. After twelve years, the naming cycle is repeated.

Look at the diagram of the Chinese zodiac. Find the year in which you were born. That is the animal, or "sign," you were born under. Some Chinese believe that people born under the sign of a certain animal will have the characteristics of that animal. Here are some of the characteristics believed to be typical of those born in each year:

Year of the Rat: An easy life for those born during the day; a hard life for those born at night, since rats sleep by day and look for food at night.

Year of the Ox: Thoughtful and patient; tries hard and does not give up easily.

Year of the Tiger: Loyal to friends; a good worker and a successful person.

Year of the Rabbit: Easily content; happy in a large family.

Year of the Dragon: Likes to be left alone; doesn't like change; enjoys nighttime.

Year of the Snake: Crafty but wise; good at many things.

Year of the Horse: Strong and friendly; gets along well with strangers.

Year of the Sheep: A leader; proud, and good at helping others in need.

Year of the Monkey: Curious and quick to learn; makes a good parent.

Year of the Chicken: Hardworking and proud; wants to succeed.

Year of the Dog: Loyal and quick to learn.

Year of the Pig: Intelligent, but also easily upset; emotional.

Chinese Zodiac Wheel:

- **RAT** — 1924, 1936, 1948, 1960, 1972, 1984
- **PIG** — 1923, 1935, 1947, 1959, 1971, 1983
- **DOG** — 1922, 1934, 1946, 1958, 1970, 1982
- **CHICKEN** — 1921, 1933, 1945, 1957, 1969, 1981
- **MONKEY** — 1920, 1932, 1944, 1956, 1968, 1980
- **SHEEP** — 1919, 1931, 1943, 1955, 1967, 1979, 1991
- **HORSE** — 1918, 1930, 1942, 1954, 1966, 1978, 1990
- **SNAKE** — 1917, 1929, 1941, 1953, 1965, 1977, 1989
- **DRAGON** — 1916, 1928, 1940, 1952, 1964, 1976, 1988
- **RABBIT** — 1927, 1939, 1951, 1963, 1975, 1987
- **TIGER** — 1926, 1938, 1950, 1962, 1974, 1986
- **OX** — 1925, 1937, 1949, 1961, 1973, 1985

Cinco de Mayo: May 5

Cinco de Mayo means "fifth of May." It is an important patriotic festival for Mexican Americans.

In 1861, Mexico owed many debts, partly from fighting with the United States over the control of Texas and California. Emperor Napoleon III sent French troops to help the Mexican government collect taxes from the people, who rebelled. The French wanted to take control of Mexico. But on May 5, 1862, they were defeated by Mexican troops at the Battle of Puebla.

Cinco de Mayo is celebrated in southwestern states such as Arizona, New Mexico, and Colorado. Parades, speeches, and spicy Mexican foods are part of the celebrating.

Colorful dancers perform in a Cinco de Mayo celebration in Denver, Colorado.

Kwanzaa

Beginning on December 26, many African American families celebrate Kwanzaa. This means "first fruits" in Swahili, an African language. The festival customs come from African harvest celebrations. Kwanzaa was first celebrated in America in the 1960s. It lasts seven days. It is a time for families to honor their African heritage and the values of family life.

On each night of Kwanzaa, families gather around a table. They light one of the seven Kwanzaa candles and talk about the importance of family life. The children receive presents, which are often homemade each night.

UNITED NATIONS DAY

The United Nations is an international peace organization created in 1945. The first United Nations Day was observed three years later, on October 24. Today, just as it did during that first celebration, the United Nations holds special seminars and rallies. Many United Nations information centers are open to the public.

The week in which October 24 falls is often observed as United Nations Week. In many schools, classes spend the week studying the dress, customs, and foods of other cultures.

Native American Day: Fourth Friday in September

The first peoples of North America had to wait a long time for a holiday in their honor. Native American Day (also called American Indian Day) is usually celebrated on the fourth Friday in September. It is not, however, celebrated in every state.

In 1914, Red Fox James rode more than four thousand miles on horseback, visiting state governors. James, a member of the Blackfoot tribe, wanted the states to observe a yearly day that honored Native Americans. Many governors supported his plan. New York was the first state to officially observe the holiday, in 1916.

Throughout the year, cultural festivals promote Native American traditions and art. For example, on July Fourth in Arizona, more than twenty tribes hold a yearly cultural festival. In Colorado, summer and fall events highlight Native American culture.

A Navajo weaver displays her craft at a Native American Day celebration.

CELEBRATING OUR EARTH

All living things on Earth share one planet. All the living and non-living things that surround each plant or animal are called its environment. What have Americans done in the past to preserve their fragile environment? What will they do in the future? This chapter looks at three holidays that celebrate keeping America "green."

Arbor Day: Celebrated at Various Times

Arbor is a Latin word meaning "tree." Arbor Day is a special day set aside to plant new trees and to think about taking care of our Earth. The founder of Arbor Day was newspaperman Julius Sterling Morton.

Opposite:
Students plant a tree together to celebrate Arbor Day.

41

Morton was born in 1832 in New York. In 1854, he moved to Nebraska, where there were few trees. Morton knew that settlers needed trees to protect them from the severe winter blizzards. He knew trees would keep the soil from blowing away and would provide fruit and shade. As senior editor of Nebraska's first newspaper, Morton used the paper to tell people about the need for trees.

In 1872, Nebraska set aside April 10 as a special tree-planting day. Over one million trees were planted on the first Arbor Day. In sixteen years, more than 300 million trees were planted in Nebraska on Arbor Day. Because of this, the state became known as the Tree Planters' State.

President Grover Cleveland named Morton his secretary of agriculture. Morton was then able to talk to people throughout the United States about the importance of planting trees.

Every state now observes Arbor Day, but not on the same day. Nebraska changed its tree-planting day to Morton's birthday, April 22. In most states, Arbor Day is the last Friday in April.

Bird Day: April 26 or During the Second Week of April

When Julius Sterling Morton was United States secretary of agriculture, he received a letter. It came from the superintendent of schools in Oil City, Pennsylvania. The letter praised the idea of Arbor Day but asked why there was no Bird Day celebration.

Julius Sterling Morton started the first Arbor Day and Bird Day celebrations.

Morton urged Americans to observe a Bird Day, too. He knew that birds are important for trees. They eat many insects that kill trees, and they help to scatter tree seeds.

The first Bird Day was observed in Oil City, in 1894. Schoolchildren studied ways to protect birds.

The idea of Bird Day was spread by the Audubon Society, which protects wild birds. The society is named after John James Audubon, a famous naturalist and artist who lived from 1785 to 1851. Many states now honor birds on Audubon's birthday, April 26. Sometimes the day is called Audubon Day instead of Bird Day. In some areas, Audubon Day and Arbor Day are observed together.

43

Earth Day: April 22

On April 22, 1970, people across the United States held the first Earth Day. They rallied to show their concern for the environment. For example, a group of demonstrators in a West Virginia town dumped litter on the courthouse steps. They felt strongly that government leaders were not working to keep America's environment clean. Students at a Florida university put a rusty car on trial for polluting the air. They sentenced the car "to death" by beating it with a sledgehammer.

Actions such as these called attention to serious environmental problems. During the early 1970s, Congress passed several environmental laws. Some of these laws, for example, said that air or water could have no more than a certain amount of harmful chemicals in it.

Since that time, more and more people have taken action at the local level to help clean up the environment. In New Jersey in 1989, a high school social studies class convinced the school board to switch from Styrofoam trays to washable dishes. On Earth Day 1990, residents of St. Louis planted ten thousand trees on the banks where the Mississippi and Missouri rivers meet.

America hasn't solved all of its environmental problems. There is still much work to be done. Cars still pollute the air. Too many trees are being cut down in the forests. Not enough people are recycling glass,

A New York man makes a point about recycling at an Earth Day celebration.

paper, and aluminum. And billions of tons of garbage still foul the land and water. Luckily, Americans have become much more concerned about environmental problems and how to solve them. And now, countries all over the world celebrate Earth Day, too. Each year, Earth Day reminds us to continue searching for ways to keep America—and all our planet—green and clean.

WHAT YOU CAN DO TO SAVE THE EARTH

You don't have to wait until April to think about saving the planet! Any time of the year is a good time to start thinking about the environment. Does your community have a recycling program? Are there groups that plant trees or clean up the beaches? Here are a few agencies you can contact to get more ideas about what you and your friends can do to get involved:

The Natural Resources Defense Council
40 West 20th Street
New York, NY 10011

Renew America
Suite 710, 1400 16th Street NW
Washington, DC 20036

Kids for Saving Earth Club
P.O. Box 47247
Plymouth, MN 55447-0247

Greenpeace
51436 U Street NW
Washington, DC 20009

To find out about helping with Earth Day activities in your area, you can call (202) 475-7751 or write to:

U.S. Environmental Protection Agency
Office of the Administrator (A101-ED)
401 M Street SW
Washington, DC 20460

Chronology

1621 Pilgrims and Indians feast together in the first Thanksgiving celebration.

July 4, 1777 First celebration of American Independence Day, in Philadelphia.

November 26, 1789 George Washington makes Thanksgiving a national holiday.

October 12, 1792 Columbus Day first celebrated as a holiday in New York City.

February 22, 1800 George Washington's birthday is first observed as a national holiday.

May 5, 1862 Mexican troops defeat the French at the Battle of Puebla, now celebrated by Mexican Americans as *Cinco de Mayo.*

May 5, 1866 The first Memorial Day celebration is held in Waterloo, New York.

April 10, 1872 Nebraska celebrates the first Arbor Day.

September 5, 1882 First Labor Day celebration is held in New York, as suggested by Peter J. McGuire.

June 14, 1889 New York schools celebrate a day in honor of the flag.

February 12, 1892 Illinois, followed by other states, begins observing Lincoln's birthday as a state holiday.

1894 Bird Day first observed in Oil City, Pennsylvania.

1914 President Woodrow Wilson asks that Flag Day be observed throughout the nation.

1916 New York is the first state to observe Native American Day, on the fourth Friday in September.

November 11, 1918 Word War I ends; called Armistice Day.

1934 President Franklin D. Roosevelt makes Columbus Day, October 12, a legal holiday.

1949 Congress officially declares June 14 as Flag Day.

1952 Constitution Day and I Am an American Day are joined to make Citizenship Day, celebrated on September 17.

1954 Armistice Day renamed Veterans Day to honor veterans of all wars.

1960s Kwanzaa, the festival of "first fruits," is first celebrated by African Americans.

April 22, 1970 Earth Day first observed nationwide.

January 15, 1983 Martin Luther King, Jr.'s birthday becomes a legal holiday.

For Further Reading

Applebaum, Diana Karter. *Thanksgiving: An American Holiday, An American History.* New York: Facts On File, 1991.

Behrens, June. *Gung Hay Fat Choy.* Chicago: Childrens Press, 1990.

Behrens, June. *Powwow.* Chicago: Childrens Press, 1990.

Lowery, Linda. *Martin Luther King Day.* Minneapolis, Minnesota: Lerner Books, 1991.

Porter, A.P. *Kwanzaa.* Minneapolis, Minnesota: Lerner Books, 1991.

Taylor, Scott. *Fiesta!* Chicago: Childrens Press, 1990.

Index

Adams, John, 10
Allies, the, 30
American Indian Day (also Native American Day), 39
Arbor Day, 41, 42, 43
Arlington National Cemetery, 27, 28, 30
Armistice Day (also Veterans Day), 30
Audubon Day, 43
Audubon, John James, 43
Audubon Society, 43

Battle of Puebla, 38
Bellamy, Francis, 13
Bells Across America, 15
Bird Day, 42
Booth, John Wilkes, 22

Chinese New Year (Yuan Tan), 36, 37
Cinco de Mayo, 38
Citizenship Day, 14, 15
Civil rights, 17
    "I Have a Dream" (speech), 18
    March on Washington, 18
    segregation, 18
    Southern Christian Leadership Conference (SCLC), 18
    Voting Rights Act, 18
Civil War, 21, 27
Cleveland, Grover, 42
Columbus, Christopher, 17, 22, 23, 24
Columbus Day, 22, 24, 25
Confederate Memorial Day, 29
Constitution, 14–15, 21
Constitution Day (also Citizenship Day), 14, 15
Continental Congress, 10, 11

Declaration of Independence, 9, 10
Decoration Day, 28

Earth Day, 45, 46
Emancipation Proclamation, 21
Emperor Napoleon III, 38
Erik the Red, 25
Eriksson, Leif, 25

Fireworks, 12, 36
Flag (U.S.)

birth of, 11
Flag Day, 6, 7, 11, 13
Franklin, Benjamin, 10

George III, 9
Gettysburg Address, 21
Grand Army of the Republic (GAR), 28
Great Silence, 30
Greenland, 25

Hale, Sara Josepha, 34, 35
Honey, George, 30
Hunter, Emma, 28

I Am an American Day (also Citizenship Day), 14, 15
Iceland, 25
Independence Day (July Fourth), 5, 6, 9, 10–11

Jefferson, Thomas, 10
July Fourth (see Independence Day)

Kids for Saving Earth Club, 45
King, Jr., Martin Luther, 17, 18
    assassination of, 19
Kwanzaa, 38

Labor Day, 13, 14
Lantern Festival, 36
Liberty Bell, 15
Lincoln, Abraham, 17, 21
    assassination of, 22
Lincoln's Birthday, 21

Martin Luther King, Jr., Day, 17–19
Memorial Day, 6, 27, 28
McGuire, Peter J., 13, 14
Morton, Julius Sterling, 41–42, 43

National holiday (definition of), 5
Native Americans, 24, 25, 33
Native American Day, 39
Natural Resources Defense Council, 45
Newfoundland, 25
Niña, 22
Norwegian Vikings, 25

Parks, Rosa, 18, 19
Phillipine Islands, 11
Pinta, 22
Presidents' Day, 22

Queen Isabella and King Ferdinand, 22

Red Fox James, 39
Renew America, 45
Revolutionary War, 20, 34
Roosevelt, Franklin D., 24

Santa María, 22
Slavery, 21
Southern Christian Leadership Conference
    (SCLC), 18

Thanksgiving, 33–34
    Bradford, Governor and, 34
    Lincoln, Abraham and, 34
    Native Americans and, 34
    Pilgrims and, 34

    Plymouth Colony and, 33, 34
    Roosevelt, Franklin and, 35
    the very first, 33
Thirteenth Amendment, 21
Tomb of the Unknowns, 31

United Nations, 39
United Nations Day, 39
United States Environmental Protection Agency
    (EPA), 45
United States Military Academy at West Point, 11

Veterans Day, 27, 30, 31
Vietnam War Memorial, 28

Washington, George, 17, 20, 34
Washington's Birthday, 20
Washington Monument, 11, 20
Wilson, Woodrow, 11
World War I, 30

Yuan Tan (*see* Chinese New Year)